I0486749

Advanced Technical Analysis For Forex

Take Your Technical Analysis To The Next Level For Greater Profits

WAYNE WALKER

Introduction

———

CONGRATULATIONS ON your personal copy of *Advanced Technical Analysis for Forex*. We continue our journey from the first book to acquire a broader and deeper understanding of technical analysis for forex. The emphasis remains on practical applications. You will be introduced to new strategies along with the know-how on how to apply them. We will also examine more advanced technical analysis indicators that can increase your money making ability.

The final chapters cover advanced *fundamental* analysis and the often overlooked area of trader psychology. These sections are a bonus to traders of all types. Thanks for choosing this book!

Chapter 1: Charting Essentials

CHARTING ESSENTIALS

Charts are a forex trader's best tool. As a trader, you will most likely use your charts more than any other available tool. Since your charts will play such a large role in your trading, it is important that you become familiar with them. The more comfortable you are with your charts, the easier it will be to become a profitable forex trader.

To help you become acquainted with charts and how you can effectively use them, we will cover the following concepts: chart setup, chart timeframes, chart types. We will also cover the useful technical indicators you can add to your charts to improve your trading results in the later chapters. We will begin with some base concepts to quickly prep you for more advanced content later.

Chart Setup

Let us start from the base and take a look at how a forex price chart is put together. Once you understand the basics, you will find it easier to apply the more advanced concepts to your technical analysis. Forex price charts are built on two axes: the X axis (horizontal axis) and the Y axis (vertical axis).

THE X AXIS RUNS HORIZONTALLY along the bottom of the chart providing a timeline for everything that has happened on the chart. The most recent price action is shown on the right side of the chart.

The Y axis runs vertically along the right side of the chart providing a price scale for the price movement on the chart. Lower prices are shown toward the bottom of the chart and the higher prices are shown toward the top of the chart.

When you combine the two axes together, you can see at what price a currency pair was trading at a particular time in the past.

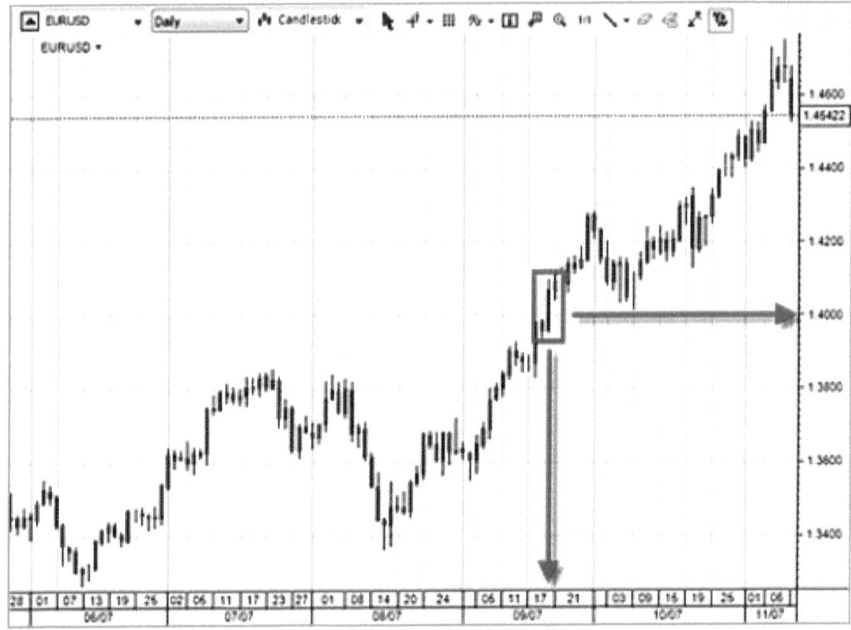

CHART TYPES

Forex charts give you the ability to analyze the price movement of a currency pair in various formats, from bar charts to candlestick charts. You have the option to select which format is best for you.

Technical analysis is a skill that traders develop, and different traders like to practice their "art" on different types of charts. Some traders believe they can see and analyze support and resistance levels better on a line chart while other traders feel they get more information on price movements on a bar or a candlestick chart. Technical analysts tend to work with the following three chart types:

Line Charts

Line charts are the most basic type of chart. Technical analysts often use line charts to quickly identify support and resistance levels. Line charts only have basic information plotted on them, which means there is not a lot of other information to cloud your analysis. You create a line chart by plotting the closing price of each trading period on a chart and then connecting each closing price with a line. You can see an example of a line chart below.

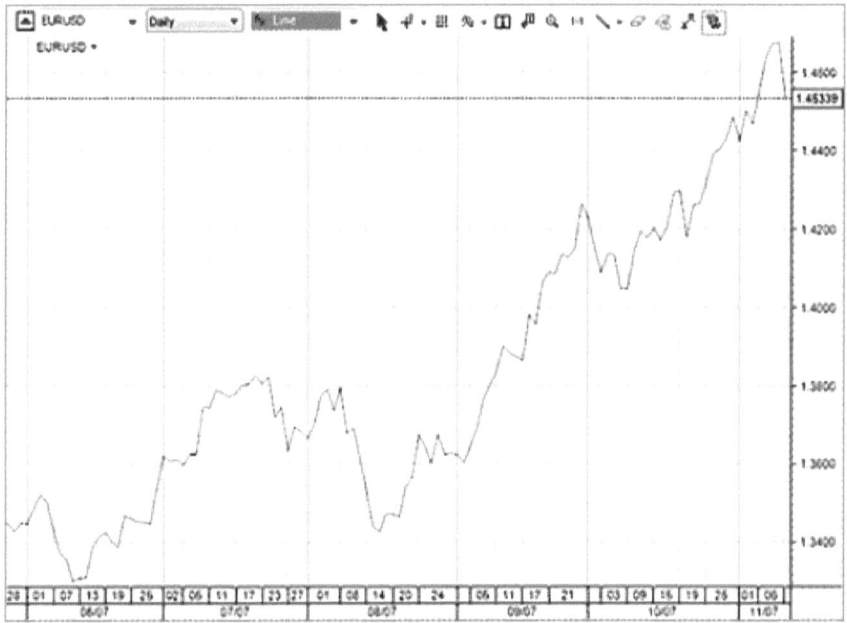

BAR CHARTS

Bar charts provide more information than a line chart. Technical traders often use bar charts to gain more information about how a currency pair's price fluctuated during each trading period. Whereas line charts only plot the closing price from each trading period, bar charts plot the opening, high, low and closing prices from each period.

You create a bar chart by plotting a series of bars across the chart. Each bar represents one trading period. To create a bar, you plot the high and low price of a trading period and connect them with a vertical line. Next, you plot the opening price out to the left side of the vertical line you have just drawn and connect that point to the vertical line with a horizontal line. Last, you plot the closing price out to the right side of the vertical line you have just drawn and connect that point to the vertical line with a horizontal line.

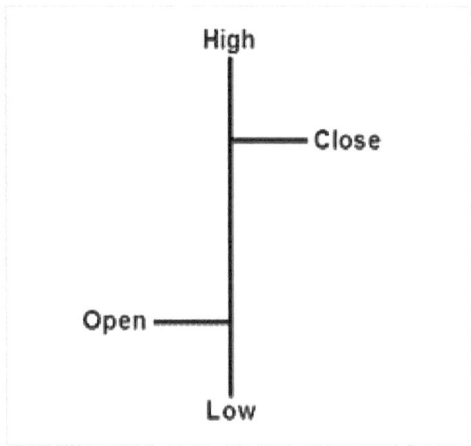

SEEING WHERE A CURRENCY pair started the trading period compared to where it ended the trading period can help you to better identify trends. If the price closes higher than it opened, you know investors were bullish on the currency pair during the trading period. If the price closes lower than it opened, you know investors were bearish on the currency pair during the trading period. You can see an example of a bar chart below.

CANDLESTICK CHARTS

Candlestick charts provide the similar information as bar charts but in a slightly different format. Technical traders many times use candlestick charts instead of bar charts because it is easier to see and identify various trading patterns using candlestick charts. In fact, a complete line of technical analysis, Japanese candlestick-chart analysis was developed around these charts.

You create a candlestick chart by plotting a series of candlesticks across the chart. Each candlestick represents one trading period. To create a candlestick, you plot the high and low price of a trading period and connect them with a vertical line. This line is called the shadow of the candle. Next, you plot the opening price by drawing a horizontal line through the vertical line, or shadow. After you have plotted the opening price, you plot the closing price by drawing another horizontal line through the vertical line. Lastly, you fill in the area between the opening price and the closing price. This area is called the body of the candlestick.

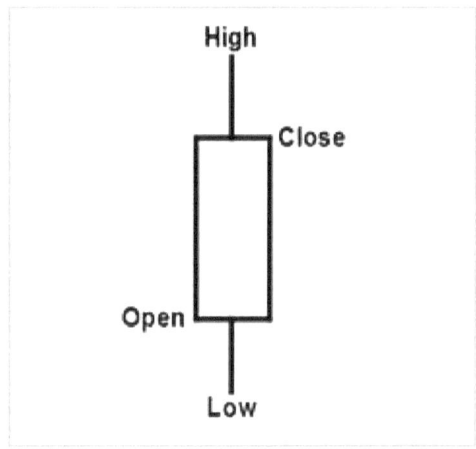

KNOWING WHERE A CURRENCY pair started the trading period compared to where it ended the trading period can help you to better identify trends. If the price closes higher than it opened, you know investors were bullish on the currency pair during the trading period. If the price closes lower than it opened, you know investors were bearish on the currency pair during the trading period.

You can see an example of a candlestick chart below.

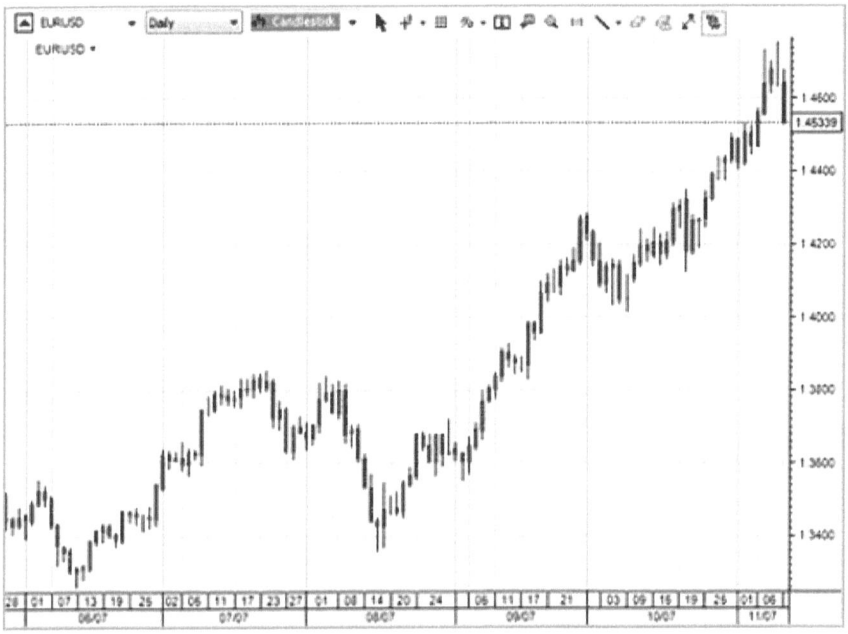

Chapter 2: Technical Indicators

TECHNICAL INDICATORS

Charts tell a market story. However, from time to time those charts may tell a story that you do not understand and you may need some help from an indicator. Technical indicators are the interpreters of the forex market. They look at price information and translate it into simple, easy to understand signals that can help you determine when to buy or when to sell a currency pair.

Technical indicators are based on mathematical equations that produce a value that is then plotted on your chart. For example, a moving average calculates the average price of a currency pair in the past and plots a point on your chart. As your currency chart moves forward, the moving average plots new points based on the updated price information it has. Ultimately, the moving average gives you a smooth indication of which direction the currency pair is moving.

EACH TECHNICAL INDICATOR provides unique information. You will find that you will naturally gravitate toward specific technical indicators based on your trading style, but it is important to become familiar with several (not all) of the technical indicators that you have available.

You should also be aware of the weaknesses associated with technical indicators: Technical indicators look at historical price data, therefore, they are not guaranteed to know anything definite about the future. Technical indicators are divided into the following categories: Trending Indicators, Oscillating Indicators, Volume Indicators.

Trending Indicators

Trending indicators, as their name suggests, identify and follow the trend of a currency pair. Forex traders are most profitable when currency pairs are trending. It is therefore crucial for you to be able to identify when a currency pair is trending and when it is consolidating. If you can enter your trades shortly after a trend begins and exit shortly after the trend ends, you will be quite successful. Let us take a look at a few trending indicators.

Moving Average

Moving averages are the most basic trending indicator. They show you in what direction a currency pair is going and where potential levels of support and resistance may be. Moving averages themselves can serve as both support and resistance. As we discuss moving averages, we will look at the following three topics: How are moving averages constructed, moving average trading signal, strengths of moving averages.

How Do You Build a Moving Average?

Moving averages are put together by finding the average closing price of a currency pair at any given time and then plotting these points on a chart. The result gives you a smooth line that follows the price movement of the currency pair.

You can manipulate the moving average by adjusting the timeframe that the indicator looks at to obtain the average price. Moving averages that look at fewer time periods to determine an average are usually more volatile. Moving averages that look at more time periods to determine an average are less volatile.

MOVING AVERAGE TRADING Signal

Moving averages provide useful entry and exit trading signals for currency pairs that are trending:

Entry signal - When a currency pair trending up bounces back up after hitting an uptrend moving average, or when a currency pair trending down pivots back down after hitting a downtrend moving average.

Exit signal - When you enter a trade on an up-trending currency pair, set a stop loss below the moving average. As the moving average rises, move your stop loss up along with the moving average. If the currency pair ever breaks far enough below the moving average, your stop loss will take you out of your trade.

When you enter a trade on a currency pair trending down, set a stop loss above the moving average. As the moving average falls, move your stop loss down along with the moving average. If the currency pair breaks far enough above the moving average, your stop loss will close your trade.

Strengths of a Moving Average

Moving averages enjoy the following strengths: They identify simple trends and are flexible enough to work in both short-term and long-term timeframes. In contrast to some indicators, they are very easy to understand.

Chapter 3: Oscillating Indicators

OSCILLATING INDICATORS

Oscillating indicators are indicators that move back and forth as currency pairs rise and fall. Oscillating indicators can help you determine how strong the current trend of a currency pair is and when that trend is in danger of losing momentum and reversing. When the oscillating indicator moves too high, the currency pair is considered to be overbought (excessive buying and there are not enough buyers left in the market to push the currency pair higher). This indicates the currency pair is at risk of a reversal or a move lower.

When an oscillating indicator moves too low, the currency pair is considered to be oversold (excessive selling and there are not enough sellers left in the market to push the currency pair lower). This indicates the currency pair is at risk of losing momentum and begin a reversal to move higher. Let's take a look at the following oscillating indicator:

Moving Average Convergence Divergence (MACD)

The moving average convergence divergence (MACD) is an oscillating indicator that can show you when a trading momentum changes from bullish to bearish and from bearish to bullish. The MACD can also reveal to you when traders are becoming exhausted, which usually results in a trend reversal for the currency pair. The MACD is usually plotted below the price movements on a chart. To learn more about the MACD we will look at the following topics: Building the MACD, MACD trading signal, Strengths of the MACD.

Building the MACD

The moving average convergence divergence is built based on a series of moving averages and how they relate to one another. The standard MACD looks at the relationship between a currency pair 12-period and 26-period exponential moving average. Specifically, the MACD looks at the distance between these two moving averages. If the 12-period moving average is above the 26-period moving average, the MACD line will be positive. If the 12-period moving average is below the 26-period moving average, the MACD line will be negative.

The MACD line is accompanied by a trigger line. This line is a 9-period exponential moving average of the MACD line.

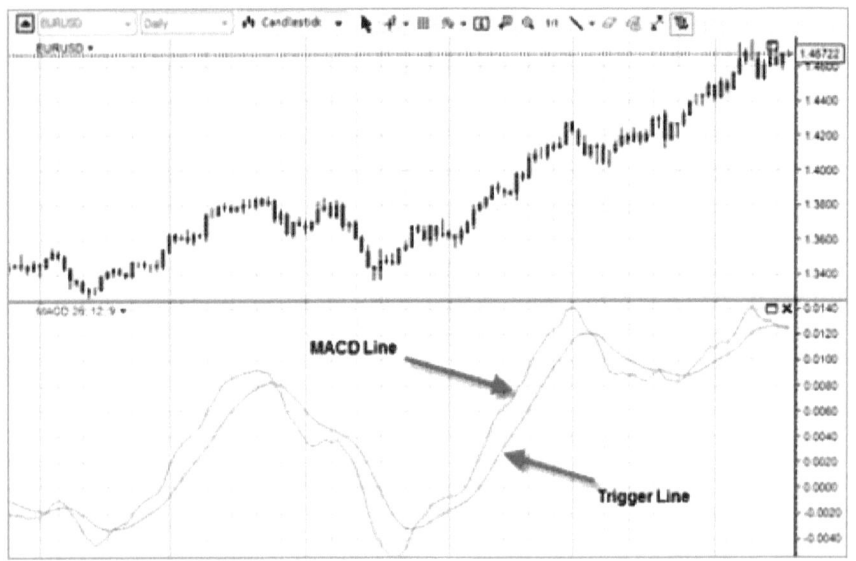

MACD TRADING SIGNAL

The moving average convergence divergence (MACD) gives trading signals as it crosses back and forth above and below the trigger line.

Entry signal - when the MACD crosses above the trigger line, you can buy the currency pair knowing that momentum has shifted from bearish to bullish. When the MACD crosses below the trigger line, you can sell the pair knowing that momentum has shifted from bullish to bearish.

Exit signal - when the MACD crosses back below the trigger line after you have bought the currency pair, you can sell the currency pair back knowing that momentum has shifted back to being bearish. When the MACD crosses back above the trigger line after you have sold the currency pair, you can buy the currency pair back knowing that momentum has shifted back to being bullish.

Strengths of the Moving Average Convergence Divergence (MACD)

The moving average convergence divergence (MACD) enjoys the following strengths: It helps you identify when the momentum of a currency pair changes and it helps you confirm the strength of current trends.

Volume Indicators

Currencies are traded on the inter-bank market and not on a central exchange, therefore, volume data for currency transactions is not available. Without volume data you cannot construct volume indicators. Therefore, we do not use volume indicators in forex trading. You can learn more about volume indicators as you diversify your trading into equities and futures.

Regional Trading Patterns

North America

Fundamentals mix very well with a combination of indicators such as RSI, MA, and MACD.

Southern Europe

Across all different markets and instruments, MAs are used to a great extent to identify trends, while RSI and Stochastic oscillators are used for momentum and sideways movements in the market.

Eastern Europe

Mostly use MACD for FX trends and Bollinger bands for sideways movements.

Northern Europe

Many Nordics trade equities and the CFD counterparts. Using the trading volume of equities, price movements can often be predicted through momentum analysis before prices change.

Chapter 4: Fibonacci Analysis

———

TECHNICAL ANALYSIS: Fibonacci

Fibonacci analysis is known for helping to identify potential support and resistance levels in the future based on past price trends and reversals. Fibonacci analysis is based on the mathematical discoveries of Leonardo Pisano also known as Fibonacci. He is credited with discovering a sequence of numbers that now bears his name, the Fibonacci sequence. The Fibonacci sequence is a series of numbers that progresses as follows, 0, 1, 1, 2, 3, 5, 8, 13, 21, 34, 55... To arrive at each subsequent number in the sequence, you simply add the two preceding numbers in the sequence. For example, to find the number that follows 55 in the sequence, you add 55 + 34 (the two preceding numbers in the sequence). The sum of 55 + 34 is 89. This is the next number in the sequence.

What grabbed Fibonacci about this sequence was not the numbers themselves but rather the relationships among the numbers, or the ratios created by various numbers in the sequence. Perhaps the most important ratio is 1.618 also known as the golden ratio. This number can be found throughout nature and throughout the Fibonacci sequence. Each number in the Fibonacci sequence is 1.618 times larger than the preceding number. For example, 89 is 1.618 times larger than 55 (89 / 55 = 1.618).

The golden ratio and the other ratios that exist within the Fibonacci sequence represent the natural ebb and flow of life. They are also applicable to the natural flow of the forex market. In this chapter, you will learn how Fibonacci ratios can be applied to forex using the following analysis tools: Fibonacci Retracements, Fibonacci Projections, Fibonacci Fans.

Fibonacci Retracements

When a currency pair pivots or reverses trend, forex traders naturally want to know how far the pair is most likely to move in its new direction. Fibonacci retracement levels can help. Certain Fibonacci ratios are useful when you are attempting to determine how far a currency pair is going to retrace against a previous trend. The ratios that you will use in your forex trading will help you find the following retracement levels:

61.8 percent — This level is found by dividing a number in the Fibonacci sequence by the number following it in the sequence (55 / 89 = 61.8%).

38.2 percent — This level is found by dividing a number in the Fibonacci sequence by the second number following it in the sequence (34 / 89 = 38.2%).

23.6 percent — This level is found by dividing a number in the Fibonacci sequence by the third number following it in the sequence (21 / 89 = 23.6%).

You will also use three other levels in your retracement analysis. While the following levels are not calculated using numbers within the Fibonacci sequence, they are based on the Fibonacci levels above:

50 percent — This level is determined by finding the middle between 61.8 percent and 38.2 percent ((61.8% + 38.2%) / 2 = 50%).

76.4 percent — This level is determined by finding the distance from 38.2 percent and 23.6 percent (38.2% - 23.6% = 14.6%) and adding it to 61.8 percent (61.8% + 14.6% = 76.4%).

100 percent — This level is determined simply by finding where the previous trend began.

Determining all six Fibonacci retracement levels provides you with potential support and resistance levels you can use in your forex trading. You can see these Fibonacci levels on the daily GBP/USD chart below. Each of the illustrated levels was calculated based on the trend highlighted by the red arrow. You could have used each level to help you determine when to enter and exit your trades as the currency pair began to turn around and move lower.

NOTICE HOW THE PRICE of the currency pair moved back and forth, bouncing off of these support and resistance levels for months until finally breaking back up above the high established by the previous trend (also known as the zero percent level) in late October.

Fibonacci Projections

Trends rarely go directly straight up or straight down. At first trends move in one direction, then they pull back and go in the opposite direction for a while and then they reverse and resume moving in the previous direction. This is the natural ebb and flow of a trend.

When a currency pair resumes its previous trend, forex traders naturally want to know how far the pair is most likely to continue moving. Fibonacci projection levels can help. Certain Fibonacci ratios are useful when you are trying to determine how far a currency pair is going to move once it resumes its previous trend. The ratios you will be using in your trading will help you find the following projection levels:

161.8 percent	This level is found by dividing a number in the Fibonacci sequence by the number immediately preceding it in the sequence (89 / 55 = 161.8%).
261.8 percent	This level is found by dividing a number in the Fibonacci sequence by the second number preceding it in the sequence (89 / 34 = 261.8%).
423.8 percent	This level is found by dividing a number in the Fibonacci sequence by the third number preceding it in the sequence (89 / 21 = 423.8%).

Determining all three Fibonacci projection levels provides you with potential support and resistance levels you can use in your forex trading.

You can see these Fibonacci levels on the daily GBP/USD chart. Each of the illustrated levels was calculated based on the trend highlighted by the red arrow. Now that the GBP/USD has resumed its up trend, you can use each level to help you determine where to set your profit targets (exit levels) as you buy this currency pair.

NOTICE THAT THE CURRENCY pair, based on the previous trend, has the potential to move up to the 161.8 percent projection level in the near future. If it reaches this level, you could set the 261.8 percent projection level as your next profit target level.

Fibonacci Fans

Fibonacci levels provide diagonal levels of support and resistance as well as horizontal levels of support and resistance. The diagonal levels of support and resistance are called Fibonacci fans. Fibonacci fans are based on three Fibonacci retracement levels 61.8 percent, 50 percent and 38.2 percent. To build a Fibonacci fan, you have to do the following:

1. Identify a trend
2. Identify the three horizontal Fibonacci levels (61.8 percent, 50 percent and 38.2 percent) as they relate to that trend
3. Draw a vertical line that crosses through these levels at the

point where the trend ended

4. Draw three lines, each one beginning where the trend began and crossing through a separate point where the vertical line intersects one of the Fibonacci levels

Now that you have your Fibonacci fans drawn, you can use them to project potential support and resistance levels that you can use in your forex trading.

You can see a Fibonacci fan on the daily GBP/USD chart below. Each of the illustrated levels was calculated based on the trend highlighted by the red arrow. You could have used the rays from the fan to help you determine when to enter and exit your trades as the currency pair began to turn around and move lower.

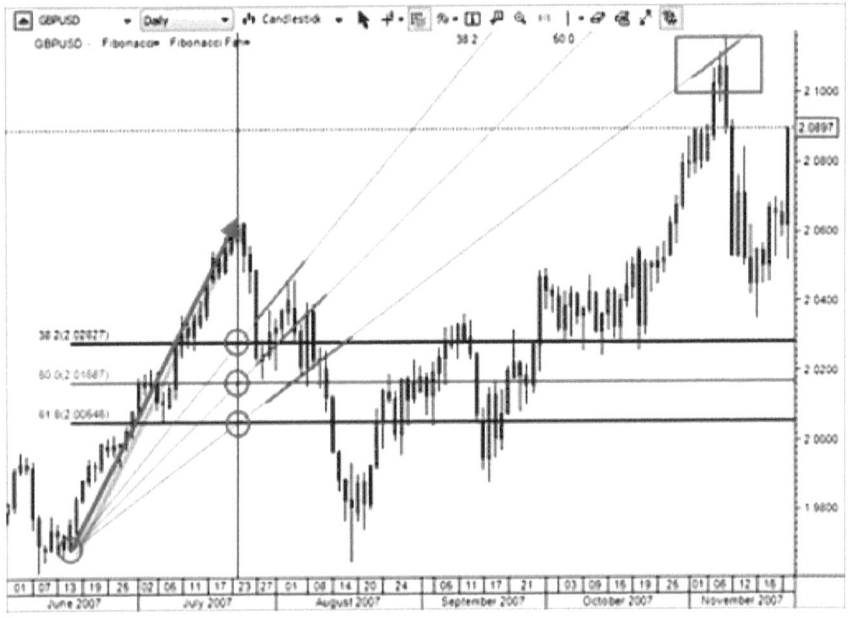

NOTICE HOW THE PRICE of the currency pair bounced off of the middle ray of the Fibonacci fan for a while in early August before it broke through that level and began bouncing off of the bottom ray of the fan for a few days. It is also interesting to see that the levels created by the Fibonacci fan continue to be a factor far into the future. You can see how the GBP/USD bounced down after hitting the bottom ray of the fan four months later in November.

Regional material: Fibonacci in USA and Europe

In Eastern Europe, Fibonacci is a popular tool for trend analysis for major forex pairs, however, many American traders use it to find support and resistance, and to trade break-outs.

In Southern Europe, Fibonacci is a very common indicator in the toolbox of seasoned traders. A sizeable amount of traders use Fibonacci to analyze break outs. In general, Fibonacci is mostly used to identify support and resistance levels in forex.

Chapter 5: Price Patterns

─────

TECHNICAL ANALYSIS: Price Patterns

Traders vote with their money. If they believe a currency pair is going to move higher, they will buy it. If they believe a currency pair is heading lower, they will sell it. When money is on the line, traders will do whatever it takes to be profitable. Oftentimes the actions of these traders form price patterns on the chart.

Price patterns are chart formations that provide insight into what forex traders are thinking at various price levels. Learning to recognize various price patterns gives you an edge over traders who are only using fundamentals or technical indicators. Imagine having the ability to precisely identify trade entry points as a currency pair breaks out and the ability to accurately project how far a currency pair is going to move once it has broken out and starts to move. Price patterns helps you with this. Price patterns are divided into the following two categories: Continuation Patterns, Reversal Patterns.

Continuation Patterns

Forex traders frequently ask themselves, "how long will this trend continue?". Deciding whether to enter a new trade in the middle of a trend or whether to exit the trade you are in and lock in your profits is difficult. You can never know if a currency pair is going to reverse and start moving in the opposite direction or can you? Continuation patterns provides you with an early warning when a currency pair is likely to continue its trend after a brief consolidation period and how far the currency pair is likely to move in that direction. Obviously, continuation patterns are not perfect, but they do increase the odds of your success. We will look at some of the well-known price continuation patterns.

Pennants

Pennants are continuation patterns that form as the price of a currency pair moves into a tighter and tighter consolidation range. Pennants can be either bullish or bearish, depending on what the trend was before the pennant began to form. If a currency pair was in an uptrend before the pennant began to form, it is a bullish continuation pattern. If a currency pair was in a downtrend before the pennant began to form, it is a bearish continuation pattern. Pennants usually form over shorter periods of time. Pennants all have the following characteristics:

Resistance level (A) - down-trending level of resistance that is converging with the support level.

Support level (B) - up-trending level of support that is converging with the resistance level.

Flagpole (C) - the trend preceding the formation of the pennant. The flagpole spans the distance from the beginning of the trend to the highest point of the pennant (bullish pennant), or the flagpole spans the distance from the beginning of the trend to the lowest point of the pennant (bearish pennant).

Breakout point (D) - the point at which the currency pair breaks up above the down-trending level of resistance (bullish pennant), or the point at which the currency pair breaks down below the up-trending level of support (bearish pennant).

Price projection (E) - the price to which the currency pair will most likely fall after it has broken out of the pennant formation (bearish pennant), or the price to which the currency pair will most likely rise after it has broken out of the pennant formation (bullish pennant). The distance the currency pair is projected to move is equal to the height of the flagpole.

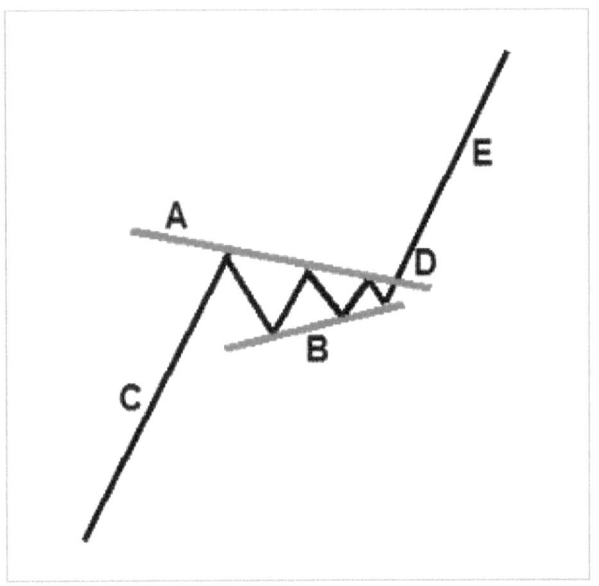

FLAGS

Flags are continuation patterns that form as the price of a currency pair pulls back from the predominant trend in a parallel channel. Flags can be either bullish or bearish, depending on what the trend was before the flag began to form. If a currency pair was in an uptrend before the flag began to form, it is a bullish continuation pattern. If a currency pair was in a downtrend before the flag began to form, it is a bearish continuation pattern. Flags usually form over shorter periods of time. Flags all have the following five characteristics:

Resistance level (A) - down-trending level of resistance that is parallel with the support level (bullish flag), or an up-trending level of resistance that is parallel with the support level (bearish flag).

Support level (B) - down-trending level of support that is parallel with the resistance level (bullish flag), or an up-trending level of support that is parallel with the resistance level (bearish flag).

Flagpole (C) - the trend preceding the formation of the flag. The flagpole spans the distance from the beginning of the trend to the highest point of the flag (bullish flag), or the flagpole spans the distance from the beginning of the trend to the lowest point of the flag (bearish flag).

Breakout point (D) - the point at which the currency pair breaks up above the down-trending level of resistance (bullish flag), or the point at which the currency pair breaks down below the up-trending level of support (bearish flag).

Price projection (E) - the price to which the currency pair will most likely fall after it has broken out of the flag formation (bearish flag), or the price to which the currency pair will most likely rise after it has broken out of the flag formation (bullish flag). The distance the currency pair is projected to move is equal to the height of the flagpole.

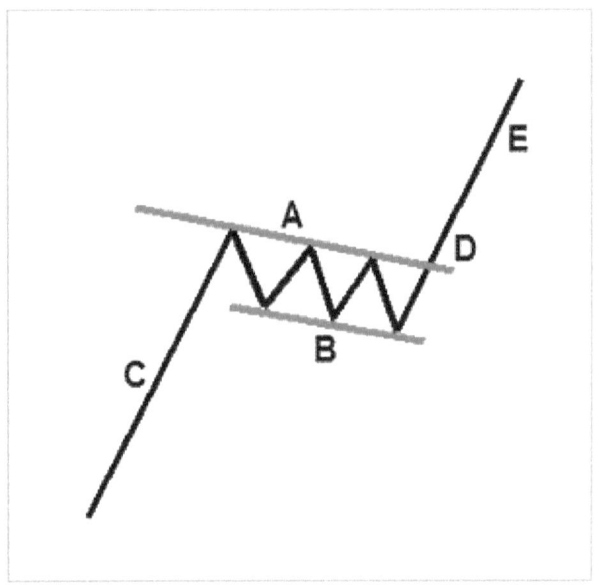

TRIANGLES

Triangles are continuation patterns that form as the price of a currency pair hits a flat level of support or resistance and begins moving into a tighter and tighter consolidation range. Triangles can be either bullish or bearish, depending on what the trend was before the wedge began to form. If a currency pair was in an uptrend before the triangle began to form, it is a bullish continuation pattern. If a currency pair was in a downtrend before the triangle began to form, it is a bearish continuation pattern. Triangles usually form over longer periods of time.

Triangles all have the following characteristics:

Resistance level (A) - horizontal level of resistance (bullish or ascending triangle), or a down-trending level of resistance that is converging with the support level (descending triangle).

Support level (B) - up-trending level of support that is converging with the resistance level (bullish or ascending triangle), or a horizontal level of support (bearish, or descending triangle).

Flagpole (C) - the trend preceding the formation of the triangle. The flag pole spans the distance from the beginning of the trend to the highest point of the triangle (bullish or ascending triangle), or the flag pole spans the distance from the beginning of the trend to the lowest point of the triangle (bearish or descending triangle).

Breakout point (D) - the point at which the currency pair breaks up above the horizontal level of resistance (bullish, or ascending triangle), or the point at which the currency pair breaks down below the horizontal level of support (bearish, or descending triangle).

Price projection (E) - the price to which the currency pair will most likely fall after it has broken out of the triangle formation (bearish or descending triangle), or the price to which the currency pair will most likely rise after it has broken out of the triangle formation (bullish or ascending triangle). The distance the currency pair is projected to move is equal to the height of the flagpole.

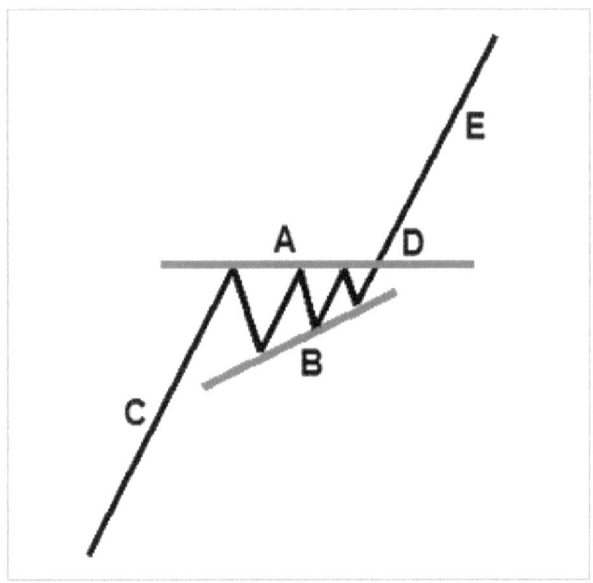

REVERSAL PATTERNS

As we already covered, forex traders often ask themselves the question, "how long will the trend continue?". Deciding whether a trend is over and if it is time to trade against the previous trend is difficult. You never know 100% if a currency pair is going to reverse and move in the opposite direction. Reversal patterns give you an early tip of when a currency pair is likely to turn around and begin a new trend and how far the currency pair is likely to move in the opposite direction. Let us review the following price reversal patterns:

Double Tops and Bottoms

Double tops and bottoms are reversal patterns that form as the price of a currency pair hits a support or resistance level twice before the pair pivots and moves in the opposite direction. Double tops are bearish reversal patterns and double bottoms are bullish reversal patterns. If a currency pair is in an uptrend, it will form a double top. If a currency pair is in a downtrend, it will form a double bottom. Double tops and bottoms usually form over longer periods of time. Double tops and bottoms have the following characteristics:

Resistance level (A) - horizontal level of resistance.

Support level (B) - horizontal level of support.

Breakout point (C) - the point at which the currency pair breaks up above the horizontal level of resistance (double bottom), or the point at which the currency pair breaks down below the horizontal level of support (double top).

Price projection (D) - the price to which the currency pair will most likely fall after it has broken out of the double-top formation, or the price to which the currency pair will most likely rise after it has broken out of the double-bottom formation.

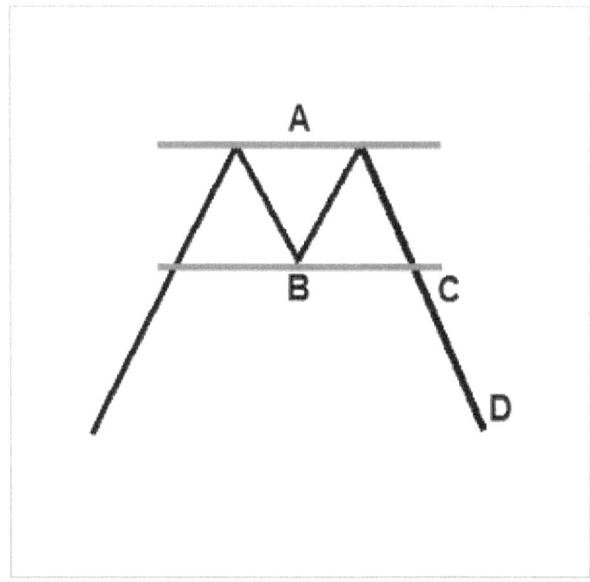

TRIPLE TOPS AND BOTTOMS

Triple tops and bottoms are reversal patterns that form as the price of a currency pair hits a support or resistance level three times before the currency pair turns around and moves in the opposite direction. Triple tops are bearish reversal patterns and triple bottoms are bullish reversal patterns. If a currency pair is in an uptrend, it will form a triple top. If a currency pair is in a downtrend, it will form a triple bottom. Triple tops and bottoms typically form over longer periods of time.

Triple tops and bottoms all have the following characteristics:

Resistance level (A) - horizontal, or slightly angled, level of resistance.

Support level (B) - horizontal, or slightly angled, level of support.

Breakout point (C) - the point at which the currency pair breaks up above the horizontal level of resistance (triple bottom), or the point at which the currency pair breaks down below the horizontal level of support (triple top).

Price projection (D) - the price to which the currency pair will most likely fall after it has broken out of the triple-top formation, or the price to which the currency pair will most likely rise after it has broken out of the triple-bottom formation.

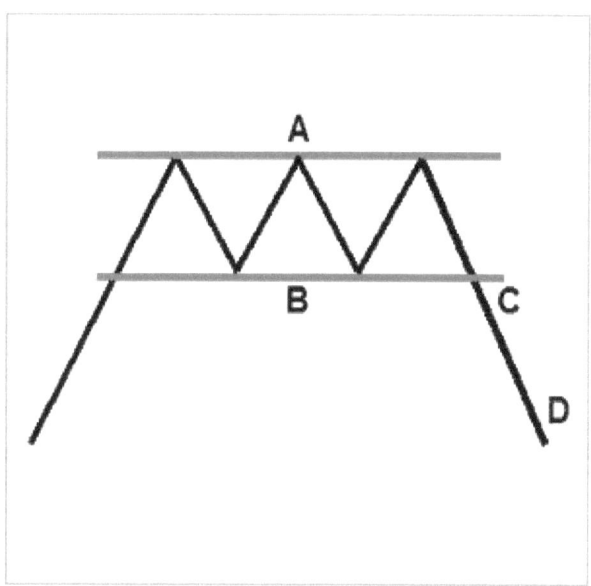

HEAD AND SHOULDERS Tops/Bottoms

Head and shoulders tops are reversal patterns that form as the price of a currency pair hits a resistance level (forming the first shoulder), then breaks through the first resistance level and hits a higher resistance level (forming the head) and then hits the first resistance level again (forming the second shoulder).

Head and shoulders bottoms are reversal patterns that form as the price of a currency pair hits a support level (forming the first shoulder), then breaks through the first support level and hits a lower support level (forming the head) and then hits the first support level again (forming the second shoulder).

Head and shoulders tops are bearish reversal patterns and head and shoulders bottoms are bullish reversal patterns. If a currency pair is in an uptrend, it will form a head and shoulders top. If a currency pair is in a downtrend, it will form a head and shoulders bottom. Head and shoulders tops or bottoms usually form over long periods of time. Head and shoulders tops or bottoms all have the following five characteristics:

Left shoulder (A) - horizontal, level of resistance (head and shoulders top), or a horizontal, or slightly angled, level of support (head and shoulders bottom).

Head (B) - higher horizontal level of resistance (head and shoulders top), or a lower horizontal, or slightly angled, level of support (head and shoulders bottom).

Right shoulder (C) - horizontal, or slightly angled, level of resistance that is in line with the left shoulder (head and shoulders top), or a horizontal level of support that is in line with the left shoulder (head and shoulders bottom).

Neckline (D) - horizontal, or slightly angled, level of support (head-and-shoulders top), or a horizontal, or slightly angled, level of resistance (head-and-shoulders bottom).

Breakout point (E) - the point at which the currency pair breaks up above the neckline (head-and-shoulders bottom), or the point at which the currency pair breaks down below the neckline (head and shoulders top).

Price projection (F) - the price to which the currency pair will most likely fall after it has broken out of the head and shoulders top formation, or the price to which the currency pair will most likely rise after it has broken out of the head-and-shoulders bottom formation. The distance the currency pair is projected to move is equal to the distance between the head and the neckline.

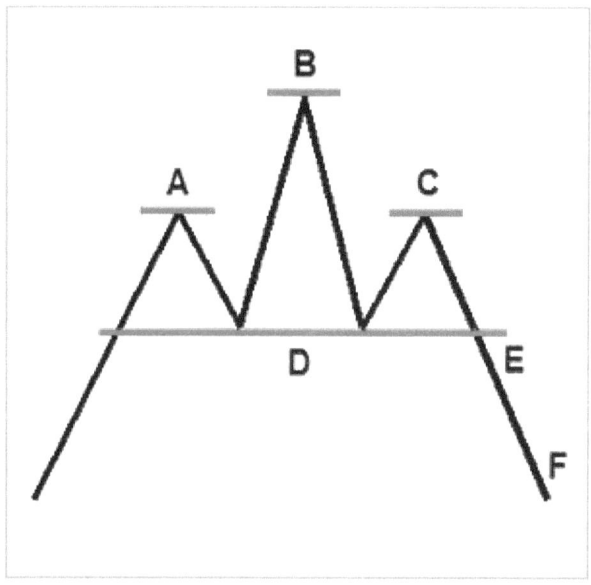

Chapter 6: Using Multiple Time Frames

———

TRADING USING MULTIPLE Time Frames

Traders of virtually every account size and risk tolerance trade the forex market. At any given moment, short-term scalpers and long-term fundamental analysis traders are looking at the same currency pairs and are trying to figure out how to place or adjust their trades. However, while they may be looking at the same currency pairs, they are not looking at the same chart timeframes. Short-term traders are most likely looking at 5-minute to 15-minute charts, while long-term traders are most likely looking at daily to monthly charts.

Trends, support and resistance lines, and technical indicators look much different on a 1-minute chart than they do on a daily chart. For example, you may look at a 1-minute chart of the EUR/USD and see that the pair appears to be in a downtrend. If you adjust your chart to a daily setting, you may see that the currency pair has been in an uptrend for weeks. So which chart is correct? Is the EUR/USD in an uptrend or a downtrend?....depends on your trading timeframe.

Forex traders trade with a bias toward the long-term trend. It has had a longer time to establish itself, and it will take a large breakout to change its direction. Obviously, if you see the fundamentals changing for a currency or a news announcement affecting a currency, you can trade against the long-term trend if you use good risk management. You should always be alert of trends and the support and resistance levels across multiple timeframes. This allows you to identify how strong various trends are. Using multiple timeframes on your charts helps you fine-tune your technical analysis.

You should analyze the following three charts in your technical analysis: Trend Chart (long term), Signal Chart, Timing Chart (short term). Once you have analyzed each timeframe, you can combine them to confirm a high-probability set up.

Trend Chart

The trend chart helps you identify the main trend that you should seek to trade with. If the currency pair in the trend chart is trending upward, you should be looking to buy the pair. If the currency pair in the trend chart is trending downward, you should be looking to sell it. To identify the timeframe that you should use for your trend chart, you first need to identify the timeframe you normally use on your trading (signal) charts. Once you have identified the timeframe of your signal chart, you should go up one timeframe to find the timeframe you should be using on your trend chart. The following is a list of common signal-chart time frames you can use to identify the appropriate time frame for your trend chart:

1-minute signal chart	=	15- to 30-minute trend chart
5-minute signal chart	=	1-hour trend chart
15- to 30-minute signal chart	=	4-hour trend chart
1-hour signal chart	=	1-day trend chart
1-day signal chart	=	1-week trend chart
1-week signal chart	=	1-month trend chart

For example, if you typically trade the EUR/USD looking at a 1-hour chart, you should use a 1-day chart for your trend chart. If you typically trade the EUR/USD looking at a 15-minute chart, you should use a 4-hour chart for your trend chart.

Once you have identified the timeframe you should use for your trend chart, all you need to do is determine what the prevailing trend on the chart is. You can use diagonal support and resistance levels or moving averages to identify the trend. You can see on our weekly EUR/USD that both the diagonal support level and the moving average indicate that this currency pair is in an uptrend.

IF THERE IS AN UPTREND on your trend chart, you should be looking for buy signals on your signal chart. If there is a downtrend on your trend chart, you should look out for sell signals on your signal chart. Once you have identified the trend, you now need to identify profitable trading signals.

Signal Chart

The signal chart is your most important chart. It provides the trading signals that tell you when to look for buying and selling opportunities based on the trading system you use. For example, if you typically use the commodity channel index (CCI) to help you identify trading signals, you will use the signal chart here. You will not use the indicator on the trend chart.

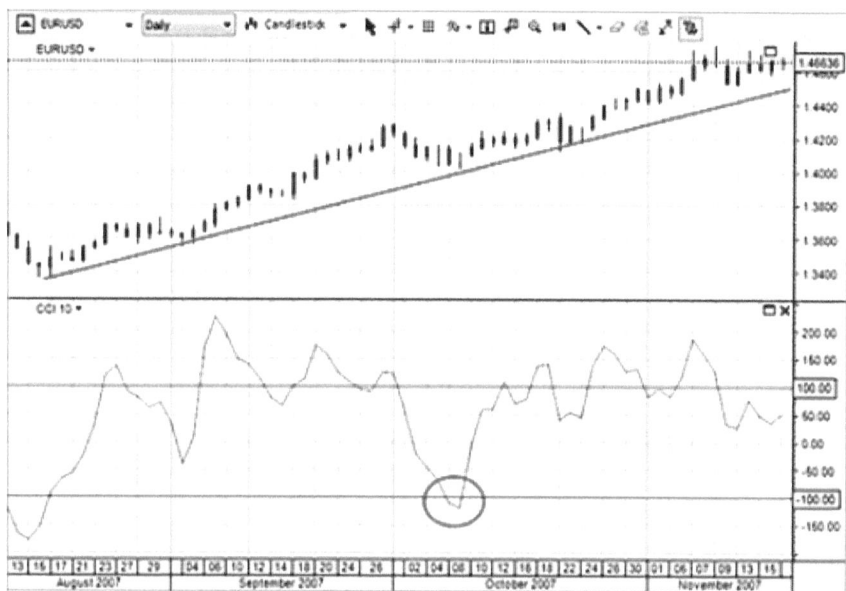

USING A SIGNAL CHART together with a trend chart allows you to more accurately identify potential profitable trade signals. For example, if your trend chart shows the currency pair is in an uptrend, you should only look for buy signals on your signal chart. The best way to take advantage of a longer-term uptrend is to buy the currency pair. If your trend chart shows the currency pair is in a downtrend, you should only look for sell signals on your signal chart. The best way to take advantage of a longer-term down trend is to sell the currency pair.

The trend chart allows you to ignore the less profitable trading signals that you see on your signal chart. Since these trading signals are going against the longer-term trend, they are most likely to be unprofitable. Now that you have identified your trading signals, you need to determine exactly when to enter and exit your trades using your timing chart.

Timing Chart

The timing chart helps you time exactly when you should enter and exit a trade. Every pip counts when you are a forex trader so the more accurate you are with your entry and exit points, the more profits you earn for your account. The following is a list of common signal chart time frames you can use to identify the best timeframe for your timing chart:

1-minute signal chart	=	Tick timing chart
5-minute signal chart	=	1-minute timing chart
15- to 30-minute signal chart	=	5-minute timing chart
1-hour signal chart	=	15-minute timing chart
1-day signal chart	=	1-hour timing chart
1-week signal chart	=	1-day timing chart
1-month signal chart	=	1-week timing chart

You can use one of the following two methods when pinpointing your entry and exit signals on your timing charts:

1. Identify the trend and support and resistance levels
2. Use the same technical indicator you use to generate your trading signals

Identify the trend plus support and resistance if you see a buy signal on your signal chart, you want to see the currency pair in an uptrend on the timing chart. You also need to see that the pair price is closer to support than it is to resistance. This tells you it has room to move higher before hitting resistance. Of course, if it has just broken up through resistance, it could continue to move higher.

If you use a technical indicator like the commodity channel index (CCI), on your signal chart to generate buy and sell signals, you can also use that same indicator on your timing chart to help you identify when to enter or exit your trade. For example, if you did use the CCI on your signal chart and it gave you a buy signal, you would add the CCI to your timing chart and make sure it was giving you a buy signal on the timing chart as well. If the CCI is not giving a buy signal on the timing chart, you should wait until it gives a buy signal on the timing chart before you enter the trade.

Chapter 7: High-Probability Trade Setup

———

HIGH-PROBABILITY TRADE Setup

Let us have a look at what a high-probability trade setup looks like using the multiple timeframe trading approach. We will analyze an example of the EUR/USD using a weekly chart as the trend chart, a daily chart as the signal chart and a 1-hour chart as the timing chart.

First, you check your trend chart to see what direction the currency is trending. As you can see on the EUR/USD weekly chart, the currency pair has been in an uptrend for a good amount of time. It would be unwise to fight this trend and attempt to sell the EUR/USD.

NEXT, YOU LOOK AT THE signal chart to identify a good buy signal for the EUR/USD. In this example, we are looking at using the commodity channel index (CCI) to generate the trading signal. You can see on the daily EUR/USD chart that the CCI gave a buy signal on October 10th as it crossed from below -100 to above -100. The trend on the daily EUR/USD chart was also moving higher.

FINALLY, YOU LOOK AT the timing chart to identify an appropriate time to buy the EUR/USD. You can see on the 1-hour EUR/USD chart that the currency pair is in an uptrend at the time the trading signal was given on the signal chart. You can also see that the CCI on the 1-hour chart had just given a buy signal at approximately the same time the CCI on the signal chart had generated its signal.

SEEING THE TRADING signal generated on the signal chart line up so well with the trend on the trend chart and the currency movement on the timing chart should give you increased confidence in the likelihood of your trade making money. Using multiple timeframes, as a rule, provides you with more accurate trading information.

Chapter 8: Intermarket Relationships

─────

INTERMARKET RELATIONSHIPS

The forex market is the most liquid financial market. While no other financial market can compete on the size of the forex market, the other markets do impact the forex market. For instance, the U.S. bond market can affect the value of the U.S. dollar (USD) just as the Canadian stock market can affect the value of the Canadian dollar (CAD).

To become a successful forex trader, you will need to understand the relationships that exist among the world's financial markets and how these relationships may affect the currency pairs you are trading. Oftentimes, you can receive an early warning of what is about to happen in the forex market by being alert of what is happening in other financial markets. For example, if you see the value of gold rising quickly, you can look for a similar rise in the value of the AUD/USD. Once you know what to be aware of you can take advantage of the similar correlations that the large institutional investors are watching. We will now focus on how the following markets affect the forex market: Commodity Market, Bond Market, Stock Market.

Commodity Market and the Forex Market

The global demand for commodities has linked the commodity market and the forex market closer. Virtually every economy around the world has to import some of its commodities. To buy these commodities, importers must exchange their currency for the currency of the economy from which they are importing the goods. This transaction drives the demand for the exporter's currency higher, which increases the value of that currency. This transaction also lowers the value of the importer's currency.

Three of the major currencies, the Canadian dollar (CAD), the Australian dollar (AUD) and the New Zealand dollar (NZD) are closely tied to commodity values because they are major commodity exporters. As the price of commodities rises, the value of these currencies normally rises. As the price of commodities falls, the value of these currencies typically falls. Each of these commodity currencies, as they are called, is affected differently by various commodities. For example, the Australian dollar is correlated with gold. As the price of gold climbs higher, the value of the Australian dollar also goes higher. As the price of gold goes lower, the value of the Australian dollar also falls. While this correlation isn't perfect, it is worth paying attention to.

Paying attention to events in the commodity market over the next years can lead you to profits in your forex trading. Be prepared to take advantage of not only the currencies that will strengthen as commodity prices increase but also of the currencies that will weaken.

Bond Market and the Forex Market

After the forex market, the global bond market is the second largest financial market in the world. Governments, institutions and individual investors all participate actively in the global bond market, and each one of these market participants is looking for the same thing, profits!

Government bonds make up the largest percentage of the global bond market. These bonds are typically viewed as risk-free investments because they are backed by the full good will and faith of national governments. However, not all government bonds are created equal. Some governments pay a higher interest rate for their bonds than others. International investors take these interest rates into account when they are deciding where to invest their money. Typically, bonds with higher interest rates are more attractive to investors as long as the economies backing the bonds are relatively stable.

Investors who wish to buy government bonds must buy these bonds with the currency of the represented government. If international investors wish to buy U.S. government bonds, they first exchange their currencies for U.S. dollars (USD). This increased demand for U.S. dollars (USD) drives the value of the USD higher. At the same time, the increased supply of international currencies on the market drives the value of these currencies lower.

Knowing which governments offer higher interest rates on their government bonds and which bonds are gaining popularity among international investors will help you know which currencies to buy and which currency to sell.

Stock Markets and the Forex Market

Individual investors globally seem to watch stock markets more closely than any other market. Stocks are exciting, they have been around for a while and most individual investors can relate to the companies in which they are buying stocks. When times are good in the stock market, money flows in. When times are bad in the stock market, money flows out.

Globalization has made it easier for investors from one country to invest in the stock markets of other countries. If investors see that stocks in the United States are performing well, they will rush to buy those stocks. If they see that stocks in Japan are starting to outperform stocks in Europe, they will take their money out of Europe and place it in Japan. Stocks are traded in the currency of the economy of which they are a part. To invest in stocks in the United States, foreign investors must first convert their currencies into U.S. dollars (USD). This increased demand for U.S. dollars drives the value of the USD higher. At the same time, the increased supply of international currencies on the market drives the value of these currencies lower.

Forex investors watch closely how the stock markets are performing. If the stock market in one country begins outperforming the stock market in another country, forex investors know that other investors are likely to move their money from the country with the weaker stock market to the country with the stronger market. This will drive the value of the currency for the country with the stronger stock market higher and the value of the currency for the country with the weaker market lower. By buying the currency from the country with the stronger market, then selling the currency from the country with the weaker market, you can potentially make a nice profit.

Chapter 9: Fundamental Analysis Essentials

―――

ECONOMIC STRENGTH BOOSTS Currency Values

Strong economies generally have strong currencies, the two are linked. When an economy is performing well, it usually means that corporations are profitable, most of the workforce is employed and, in most cases, interest rates are increasing. These characteristics of a strong economy benefits you as a forex trader.

Rising interest rates are one of the most predictive indicator for rising currency values and central banks around the world determine interest rates in their respective economies. These central banks typically raise interest rates when inflation as measured by the consumer price index (CPI) and the producers' price index (PPI) starts growing too quickly.

Economic growth gives birth to inflation. The basics are, the stronger the economy is, the higher the demand for workers becomes. As the demand for workers goes up, wages for those workers also increases. The more money workers take home in their paychecks, the more money they have to spend at retail stores, on cars and on houses. As demand for goods and services increases, the price for those goods and services also increases, in other words, inflation.

Naturally, if central banks watch inflation indicators (like the CPI and PPI) in their decision-making process, you would assume they would also be interested in watching economic strength indicators to see how strong an economy is and they most certainly are. Central banks watch the following fundamental economic indicators to gauge the strength of an economy, and so should you:

Gross Domestic Product (GDP), Non-Farm Payrolls, Durable Goods Orders, Retail Sales.

Gross Domestic Product (GDP)

The Gross Domestic Product (GDP) is the broadest measure of aggregate economic activity available. Reported quarterly, GDP growth is broadly followed as the primary indicator of economic strength.

GDP represents the total value of a country's production during the period and consists of the purchases of domestically produced goods and services by individuals, businesses, foreigners and the government. Since GDP reports are often subject to noticeable quarter-to-quarter volatility and revisions, it is best to follow the indicator on a year-to-year basis. It can be valuable to follow the trend rate of growth in each of the major categories of GDP to determine the strengths and weaknesses in the economy. A high GDP figure is often associated with the expectations of higher interest rates, which is frequently positive, at least in the short term for the currency involved. This remains true unless expectations of increased inflation pressure is simultaneously undermining confidence in the currency.

Non-Farm Payrolls(USA)

This report is a measure of the number of people employed by non-farm businesses. Monthly changes in payroll employment reflect the net number of new jobs created or lost during the month and changes are widely followed as an important indicator of economic activity.

Payroll employment is one of the primary monthly indicators of aggregate economic activity because it encompasses every major sector of the economy. It is also useful to examine trends in job creation in several industry categories because the aggregate data can mask significant deviations in underlying industry trends. Large increases in payroll employment are seen as signs of strong economic activity that could eventually lead to higher interest rates that are supportive of the currency. If inflationary pressures are seen as building, this may undermine the longer term confidence in the currency.

Durable Goods Orders

Durable Goods Orders are a major indicator of manufacturing sector trends because the majority of industrial production is done to order. Often, the indicator excludes defense and transportation orders because these are generally much more volatile than the rest of the orders and can obscure the more important underlying trend.

Durable Goods Orders are also a measure of the new orders placed with domestic manufacturers for immediate and future delivery of factory hard goods. Monthly percent changes reflect the rate of change of such orders. Levels of, and changes in durable goods order are widely followed as an indicator of factory sector momentum. Rising Durable Goods Orders are normally associated with stronger economic activity and can therefore lead to higher short-term interest rates that are often supportive to a currency.

Retail Sales

Retail Sales are a measure of the total receipts of retail stores. Monthly percentage changes reflect the rate of change of such sales and are widely followed as an indicator of consumer spending. Retails Sales are a major indicator of consumer spending because they account for nearly one-half of total consumer spending and approximately one-third of aggregate economic activity.

Often, Retail Sales are followed minus auto sales because these are generally much more volatile than the rest of the Retail Sales and can therefore obscure the more important underlying trend.

Rising Retail Sales are often associated with a strong economy and therefore an expectation of higher short-term interest rates that are often positive for a currency in the short term.

Regional Economic indicators

Regional indicators like the Tankan reports are very important for JPY, and therefore have considerable impact on other markets in the region. Machine orders are also a critical piece of data since this affects exporting companies which in turn also affects the currency.

CPI figures from various countries especially Australia, Japan and China are usually a market mover and are closely watched by professional traders.

Purchasing Manager Index (PMI) numbers set the tone for the month and are an early indicator of economic activity in the region.

Chapter 10: Trading Psychology

―――

TRADING PSYCHOLOGY

Forex traders have to not only compete with other traders in the forex market but also with themselves. Often as a forex trader, you will be your own worst enemy. As humans, we are often emotional. Our egos want to be validated, we want to prove to ourselves that we know what we are doing and that we are capable of taking care of ourselves. Our emotions and instincts can combine to provide us with trading successes every now and then. Most of the time, however, our emotions get the best of us and lead us to trading losses unless we learn to control them.

Many forex traders believe it would be ideal if you could completely separate yourself from your emotions. Unfortunately, that is very difficult, almost impossible, and some of your emotions may actually help improve your trading. The smart thing you can do is learn to understand yourself as a trader. Identify your strengths and your weaknesses, then select a trading style that is best for you. In this chapter, we will learn about the following four psychological biases that may be affecting your trading results and what you can do to overcome them: Overconfidence Bias, Anchoring Bias, Confirmation Bias, Loss Aversion Bias.

Overconfidence Bias

Overconfidence bias is an over-inflated belief in your skills as a forex trader. If you ever find yourself thinking that you have got everything figured out, there is nothing more to learn and money is yours for the taking in the market, you probably suffer from an overconfidence bias.

Dangers of Overconfidence

Overconfident traders tend to get themselves into trouble by trading too frequently (overtrading) or by placing extremely large trades as they go for the big win. In the end, an overconfident trader will end up either trading excessively, churning the trader's account or risking too much on the one trade that goes bad and wipes out most of their account balance.

Are You Overconfident?

If you want to know if you have any overconfidence tendencies, ask yourself if you have ever jumped right back into a trade you had just closed, not because you saw another entry opportunity, but because you could not believe that you were wrong? You can also consider if you have ever put more on a trade than you normally would just because you were sure the trade was going to be a winner? If you have, you need to be aware of those tendencies.

Overcoming Overconfidence

The best way to overcome an overconfidence bias is to establish a strict set of risk-management rules. These rules should at a minimum cover how many trades you will allow yourself to be in at one time, how much of your account you are willing to risk on any one trade and how much of your account are you willing to lose before you take a break from trading and evaluate your strategy. By limiting the number of trades you are willing to be in and the amount of risk you are willing to take, you can spread your risk out over your portfolio. Make failure survivable!

Anchoring Bias

Anchoring bias is a tendency to believe that the future is going to look or behave similar to the present. When you anchor yourself too closely to the present, you fail to see the dramatic changes that are possible as currency pairs fluctuate and the underlying fundamentals shift.

Dangers of Anchoring

Anchored traders usually get themselves into trouble by convincing themselves that the current trend will never end and a reversal in the economic strength of a particular country is next to impossible. Soon, they become emotionally attached to the previous trend of a currency pair and they continue to place trades that go against the new trend. With each trade they lose increasing amounts of money because they are bucking the trend.

Are You Anchoring?

If you want to know if you have any anchoring tendencies, question yourself, if you have ever lost money because you could not accept that the trend had ended. If you have, you need to be aware of that tendency.

Overcoming Anchoring

A good way to overcome anchoring is to look at multiple timeframes on your charts. If you usually trade on hourly charts, have a look at the daily and weekly charts occasionally to see where some of the longer-term levels of support and resistance are and what the long-term trends look like. You should also have a look at the shorter-term charts to see when the shorter-term trends are reversing. Expanding your perspective will help you avoid anchoring yourself to any one point.

Confirmation Bias

Confirmation bias is a propensity to look only for the information that confirms the beliefs that you already have. For instance, if you believe the EUR/USD is going to go up, you will seek the news, the technical indicators and the fundamental factors that support your belief.

Dangers of Seeking Confirmation

Traders who actively pursue confirmation of their beliefs tend to miss key warning signs that would have normally protected them from unnecessary losses. In an attempt to build a case for their beliefs, traders miss the facts. Ultimately, this leads to them fighting the trend and losing money with their trades.

Do You Seek Confirmation?

If you want to know if you have any confirmation bias tendencies, reflect on how often do you look for signs that you may be wrong in your analysis? If your answer is rarely or never, you may be a confirmation seeker, and you need to be aware of that.

Overcoming Confirmation Bias

One way to overcome confirmation bias is to find someone, or a network you can talk to about your trading. Hopefully the person or group that you talk with about your trading will not always agree with you. Speaking with traders who have diverse perspectives and ideas will help you look at your trades from different angles. Sometimes you will strengthen your convictions by talking with other traders. Other times, chatting with your trading partners will cause you to change course. Keeping an open mind will help you learn new strategies and avoid holding on too long to old beliefs.

Loss Aversion Bias

Loss aversion bias is based on the theory that the pain caused by losing $1,000 is greater than the joy that comes from gaining $1,000. To be more direct, fear is a more powerful motivator than greed.

Dangers of Loss Aversion

Traders who fear losses are much more likely to hold onto losing positions than traders who are able to accept short-term losses and move onto other more-profitable trades. Holding onto losing positions damages the stability of your account, not only by incurring losses, but it also keeps you out of better trades.

Do You Fear Losses?

If you want to know if you have any loss aversion weakness, ask yourself if you have ever held onto a losing trade past the point where you knew that you should have gotten out because you hoped the pair would turn around and erase the losses. If you have, you need to be aware of those tendencies.

Overcoming Loss Aversion

A good way to overcome a loss aversion bias is to trade with set stop-loss orders. Many traders tell themselves that they will trade with a mental stop-loss, a stop- loss that they think about and promise themselves they will execute if the currency pair ever reaches it. All too often, traders ignore this and fail to act on their mental stop-losses. They allow their emotions to dominate and they begin rationalizing their choice to stay in the trade until it turns around. As soon as you enter a trade, you must set your stop-loss order. Remove your emotions from the picture.

Conclusion

THANK YOU FOR MAKING it through to the end of *Advanced Technical Analysis for Forex*. Let's hope it was informative and able to provide you with the tools that you need to achieve your goals of trading forex and making money. The next step is to test your skills at trading and build up your risk capital. This will give you the motivation that you need to succeed.

I have several other books on different aspects of trading and asset classes please check them out!

Profile of the Author

WAYNE WALKER is the director of a global capital markets education and consulting firm (gcmsonline.info). He has several years experience in leading and coaching teams of Investment Advisors and has managed top performing teams in the Private Client Group based on Bench Mark Earnings (BME).

Don't miss out!

Visit the website below and you can sign up to receive emails whenever Wayne Walker publishes a new book. There's no charge and no obligation.

https://books2read.com/r/B-A-QSGG-ADBT

BOOKS 2 READ

Connecting independent readers to independent writers.